This book belongs to:

_____

_____

_____

_____

GOODWORD

Goodword Books Pvt. Ltd.
P. O. Box 3244, Nizamuddin P. O.,
New Delhi-110 013
E-mail: info@goodwordbooks.com
Printed in India
Illustrated by Achla Anand
First published 2005   Reprinted 2006
© Goodword Books 2006

www.goodwordbooks.com

FAVOURITE TALES FROM THE QURAN

TWO TALES:

The Iron Wall
The Queen of Egypt

Saniyasnain Khan

GOODWORD

The Iron Wall

SURAH KAHF 18:83-98

Long long ago, during the sixth century
B.C. there was a magnificent king
whose name was Dhul Qarnayn. He
made military conquests from the
Aegean Sea to the Indus River. His
sway extended over East and West.

He was just and righteous, protecting the weak and punishing the law-breakers. When Dhul Qarnayn took his armies to the North-East of Iran, he reached the Caucasus mountain range which runs between the Caspian and the Black Seas.

On these journeys he met different tribes
in different places. Once he met a tribe
whose members were hardly able to
communicate with him.

Once, in that region, he met a tribe who begged him to protect them from the wild tribes, the Yajuj and the Majuj (Gog and Magog) who kept coming through the mountain passes, and attacking them.

Dhul Qarnayn said, "Lend me a body
of men, and I will raise a wall
between you and them. Come, bring
me blocks of iron."

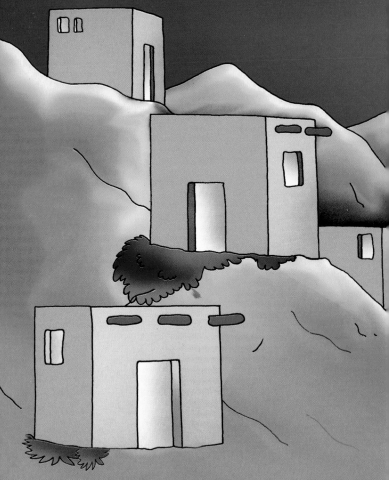

He told them to ply their bellows and
when the iron blocks which they brought
became red hot, Dhul Qarnayn asked
them to pour molten brass on them.

In this way he helped in damming up the valley between the two mountains. In this way, Dhul Qarnayn erected an Iron Wall to save them from Yajuj and Majuj.

After conquering a major part of the then inhabited world and building an iron wall, Dhul Qarnayn lost none of his humility.

He gave the entire credit for these feats to the blessing of Allah. Of the iron wall he had built, he said:

"This is a blessing from my Lord. But when the promise of my Lord will come to pass, He will make it to dust. And the promise of my Lord is true."

The Queen of Egypt

SURAH TA HA 20:38-40; AL-QASAS 28:7-13

Long, long ago a tribe called the
Children of Israel lived in Egypt. At
that time, Egypt was ruled by a cruel
King. He was called the Firawn, or
Pharaoh.

He made the Children of Israel his slaves.
He made them do hard labour. One day, a
soothsayer told the Firawn that a boy born
into the Children of Israel would destroy
him and his kingdom.

When the Firawn heard this, he ordered
the killing of all the new-born boys of
the Children of Israel. Only their
daughters were to be spared.

During these hard times, there lived a pious woman of the Children of Israel. Her name was Yukabid, and Imran was her husband. She gave birth to a beautiful boy named Moses or Musa علیه السلام.

Musa's parents felt afraid of the cruel soldiers of the Firawn. The soldiers would kill little Musa عليه السلام too. But something unusual happened.

Allah told Yukabid that her child was very special. He would one day become a great prophet. Allah promised her that the baby would be safe. He would also be returned to her.

To save the baby Musa ﷺ, his mother put him in a box and floated him down the river. As the box floated down the river, Musa's sister Miriam kept a watch on him.

The box sailed along gently. It stopped at a bank near the royal palace. Now, the Queen of Egypt was a good and kind-hearted woman.

When she saw the helpless baby, she felt great pity for him. She decided to keep the baby in the palace. She wanted to bring him up as her own child. And so baby Musa عليه السلام was saved.

This story teaches us that we should be kind and gentle towards others.

ﷺ *Alayhis Salam* 'May peace be upon him.'
The customary blessing on the prophets.